DAD JOKES

YOU NEVER ASKED FOR

400 Ways
to Make Anyone Groan

Introduction

You're holding in your hands exactly what you never knew you needed: 400 dad jokes, each cheesier than the last, guaranteed to make you groan, roll your eyes, and—dare we say it?—maybe even laugh (against your will, of course). You see, dad jokes aren't about being clever. They're about being so painfully obvious that you just can't help but love them... or at least tolerate them for a moment before questioning your life choices.

This collection is perfect for those brave enough to gift it to others, ensuring that every family dinner, car ride, or awkward conversation has a punchline—whether anyone wants it or not. These jokes will land with a thud, linger in the air, and then... hit you right where it counts (the funny bone, that is). After all, why say something profound when you can say something profoundly ridiculous?

So, flip the page, prepare to facepalm, and remember: you're about to embark on a journey of humor so "bad" that it might just be... genius? Either way, it's too late to turn back now.

Enjoy. Or don't. (But you will).

Knock, knock.
Who's there?
Boo.
Boo who?
Don't cry, it's just a joke!

Why don't skeletons fight each other?
They don't have the guts.

I only know 25 letters of the alphabet.
I don't know y.

Knock, knock.
Who's there?
Dishes.
Dishes who?
Dishes the police, open up!

What did the ocean say to the beach?
Nothing, it just waved.

I used to play piano by ear,
But now I use my hands.

Knock, knock.
Who's there?
Tank.
Tank who?
You're welcome!

Why don't eggs tell jokes?
They'd crack each other up.

I'm reading a book about anti-gravity.
It's impossible to put down.

Knock, knock.
Who's there?
Doctor.
Doctor who?
Exactly!

Did you hear about the mathematician
who's afraid of negative numbers?
He'll stop at nothing to avoid them.

Why don't some couples go to the
gym?
Because some relationships don't work
out.

Knock, knock.
Who's there?
Europe.
Europe who?
No, YOU'RE a poo!

I used to hate facial hair...
But then it grew on me.

Why don't crabs give to charity?
Because they're shellfish.

Knock, knock.
Who's there?
Annie.
Annie who?
Annie body home?

Knock, knock.
Who's there?
Harry.
Harry who?
Harry up, it's cold out here!

Want to hear a joke about
construction?
I'm still working on it.

I invented a new word!
Plagiarism.

Why did the scarecrow win an
award?
Because he was outstanding in his
field!

Why did the golfer bring two pairs of pants?
In case he got a hole in one.

Did you hear about the restaurant on the moon?
Great food, no atmosphere.

Knock, knock.
Who's there?
Cargo.
Cargo who?
Cargo beep beep!

What do you call fake spaghetti?
An impasta!

My wife told me to stop impersonating a flamingo…
I had to put my foot down.

Knock, knock.
Who's there?
Hawaii.
Hawaii who?
I'm good, Hawaii you?

Why can't you give Elsa a balloon?
Because she'll let it go.

Parallel lines have so much in common.
It's a shame they'll never meet.

Knock, knock.
Who's there?
A little old lady.
A little old lady who?
Wow, I didn't know you could yodel!

Why do cows have hooves instead of feet?
Because they lactose.

Did you hear the rumor about butter?
Well, I'm not going to spread it!

Knock, knock.
Who's there?
Bison.
Bison who?
Bison groceries on the way home.

What do you call cheese that isn't yours?
Nacho cheese!

I only drink on two occasions:
When it's my birthday and when it's not.

Knock, knock.
Who's there?
At.
At who?
Atchoo! Bless you!

Why did the coffee file a police report?
It got mugged.

I told my wife she was drawing her eyebrows too high.
She looked surprised.

Knock, knock.
Who's there?
Lettuce.
Lettuce who?
Lettuce in, it's cold out here!

How does a penguin build its house?
Igloos it together.

Want to hear a joke about paper?
Never mind, it's tearable.

Knock, knock.
Who's there?
Candice.
Candice who?
Candice door open, or what?

Why don't skeletons fight each other?
They don't have the guts.

I used to be a baker,
But I couldn't make enough dough.

Knock, knock.
Who's there?
Howard.
Howard who?
Howard you like to be out here in the
cold?

**What do you call an alligator in a vest?
An investigator.**

**I got my wife a fridge for her birthday.
I can't wait to see her face light up
when she opens it.**

**Knock, knock.
Who's there?
A broken pencil.
A broken pencil who?
Never mind, it's pointless.**

**How do you organize a space party?
You planet.**

Knock, knock.
Who's there?
Dwayne.
Dwayne who?
Dwayne the bathtub, I'm drowning!

Why did the bike fall over?
It was two-tired.

I'm terrified of elevators,
So I'm going to start taking steps to
avoid them.

Knock, knock.
Who's there?
Isabel.
Isabel who?
Isabel broken? I had to knock!

I'm reading a book on the history of glue...
I can't seem to put it down.

Why don't scientists trust atoms?
Because they make up everything!

Knock, knock.
Who's there?
Alpaca.
Alpaca who?
Alpaca the suitcase, you load the car!

I would tell you a joke about an elevator,
But it's an uplifting experience.

Knock, knock.
Who's there?
Says.
Says who?
Says me, that's who!

How does a vampire start a letter?
Tomb it may concern...

Knock, knock.
Who's there?
Orange.
Orange who?
Orange you glad I didn't say banana?

I don't trust stairs.
They're always up to something.

Knock, knock.
Who's there?
Donut.
Donut who?
Donut forget to lock the door!

What did one plate say to the other?
Lunch is on me.

Knock, knock.
Who's there?
Cows go.
Cows go who?
No, silly, cows go moo!

I have a fear of speed bumps,
But I'm slowly getting over it.

Knock, knock.
Who's there?
To.
To who?
Actually, it's "to whom."

I made a pencil with two erasers...
It was pointless.

Knock, knock.
Who's there?
Robin.
Robin who?
Robin you, now hand over the cash!

What's orange and sounds like a
parrot?
A carrot.

I'm on a seafood diet...
I see food and I eat it.

Knock, knock.
Who's there?
Iva.
Iva who?
Iva sore hand from knocking!

My wife asked me to sync her phone,
So I threw it in the ocean.

Knock, knock.
Who's there?
Butter.
Butter who?
Butter open up or I'm leaving!

How does a scientist freshen their breath?
With experi-mints.

Knock, knock.
Who's there?
Needle.
Needle who?
Needle little help here!

I'm afraid of the calendar.
Its days are numbered.

Knock, knock.
Who's there?
Lettuce.
Lettuce who?
Lettuce in, it's freezing out here!

I used to be addicted to the hokey pokey,
But then I turned myself around.

Knock, knock.
Who's there?
Olive.
Olive who?
Olive you and I miss you!

Why can't your nose be 12 inches long?
Because then it'd be a foot!

Knock, knock.
Who's there?
Anita.
Anita who?
Anita ride home!

Why did the tomato turn red?
Because it saw the salad dressing!

Knock, knock.
Who's there?
Boo.
Boo who?
Don't cry, it's just a joke!

Did you hear about the kidnapping at
school?
It's fine, he woke up.

Knock, knock.
Who's there?
Turnip.
Turnip who?
Turnip the heat, I'm freezing!

What's brown and sticky?
A stick.

Knock, knock.
Who's there?
Snow.
Snow who?
Snow way I'm telling you!

What do you call a factory that makes
good products?
A satisfactory.

Knock, knock.
Who's there?
Alaska.
Alaska who?
Alaska my mom, she might know.

Why did the math book look sad?
Because it had too many problems.

Knock, knock.
Who's there?
Broccoli.
Broccoli who?
Broccoli doesn't have a last name, silly!

I don't play soccer because I enjoy the sport,
I'm just doing it for kicks.

Knock, knock.
Who's there?
Atch.
Atch who?
Bless you!

What do you call a bear with no teeth?
A gummy bear.

Knock, knock.
Who's there?
Radio.
Radio who?
Radio not, here I come!

I told my computer I needed a break,
And now it won't stop sending me Kit-Kat ads.

Knock, knock.
Who's there?
Orange.
Orange who?
Orange you glad I didn't say banana?

What do you call a snowman with a six-pack?
An abdominal snowman.

Knock, knock.
Who's there?
Ice cream.
Ice cream who?
Ice cream if you don't let me in!

Why don't vampires go to barbecues?
They don't like steak.

Knock, knock.
Who's there?
Al.
Al who?
Al be seeing you later!

Knock, knock.
Who's there?
Who.
Who who?
Wow, I didn't know you were an owl!

Did you hear about the guy who
invented Lifesavers?
He made a mint.

What did one toilet say to the other?
You look flushed.

I'm terrified of my fridge...
Every time I open it, there's a little light
inside!

Knock, knock.
Who's there?
Harry.
Harry who?
Harry up, I'm hungry!

Why did the toilet paper roll down the hill?
To get to the bottom.

I once told a chemistry joke...
But there was no reaction.

Knock, knock.
Who's there?
Dewey.
Dewey who?
Dewey have to keep doing this?

Why did the cookie go to the hospital?
Because it felt crummy.

I'm reading a book about noses.
It's a real page-turner.

Knock, knock.
Who's there?
Ice cream soda.
Ice cream soda who?
Ice cream soda people can hear me!

What do you call a fish with no eyes?
Fsh.

My wife told me I should do lunges to stay in shape.
That would be a big step forward.

Knock, knock.
Who's there?
Water.
Water who?
Water you doing in there?

How does a dog stop a video?
It presses paws.

I didn't like my beard at first.
But then it grew on me.

Knock, knock.
Who's there?
Salad.
Salad who?
Salad you're not opening the door for me!

Why don't crabs share their food?
Because they're shellfish.

I bought some shoes from a drug dealer once...
I don't know what he laced them with, but I've been tripping all day.

Knock, knock.
Who's there?
Toby.
Toby who?
Toby continued...

Did you hear about the claustrophobic astronaut?
He needed a little space.

What do you call a pile of cats?
A meow-tain.

Knock, knock.
Who's there?
Snow.
Snow who?
Snow use, I forgot the punchline.

Why don't skeletons ever go trick-or-treating?
Because they have no body to go with

I asked my dog what's two minus two...
He said nothing.

Knock, knock.
Who's there?
Donkey.
Donkey who?
Donkey ask me, I don't know either.

Did you hear about the chameleon
who couldn't change color?
He had a reptile dysfunction.

I used to be a banker, but I lost interest.
Now I'm counting on better things.

Knock, knock.
Who's there?
Achoo.
Achoo who?
Achoo glad I didn't sneeze on you?

Why don't seagulls fly over the bay?
Because then they'd be bagels.

I tried to make a belt out of watches...
But it was a waist of time.

Knock, knock.
Who's there?
Alpaca.
Alpaca who?
Alpaca the bags, we're leaving!

What's brown and rhymes with
Snoop?
Dr. Dre.

Why don't fish play basketball?
Because they're afraid of the net.

Knock, knock.
Who's there?
Justin.
Justin who?
Justin time for more bad jokes!

I bought a ceiling fan the other day...
Complete waste of money. All it does is
sit there and clap.

Did you hear about the cheese factory
that exploded?
There was nothing left but de-brie.

Knock, knock.
Who's there?
Figs.
Figs who?
Figs the doorbell, it's broken!

Why do chickens sit on eggs?
Because they don't have chairs.

I once made a pencil with two
erasers...
It was pointless.

Knock, knock.
Who's there?
Henrietta.
Henrietta who?
Henrietta big breakfast today!

Why did the grape stop in the middle
of the road?
Because it ran out of juice.

I only know one joke about butter...
But I'm not gonna spread it.

Knock, knock.
Who's there?
Mikey.
Mikey who?
Mikey won't fit through the keyhole!

Why was the broom late?
It swept in.

Knock, knock.
Who's there?
Frank.
Frank who?
Frank you for listening to my terrible
jokes!

What's orange and sounds like a
parrot?
A carrot.

I stayed up all night wondering where
the sun went...
Then it dawned on me.

Why are elevator jokes so classic and good?
They work on many levels.

Knock, knock.
Who's there?
Omelette.
Omelette who?
Omelette smarter than you think!

Why did the toilet paper cross the road?
Because it was on a roll.

My son asked me if I could make a sandwich...
So I said, "Abracadabra, you're a sandwich!"

Knock, knock.
Who's there?
Dwayne.
Dwayne who?
Dwayne the tub, I'm drowning!

Why did the man put his money in the blender?
Because he wanted to make some liquid assets.

Knock, knock.
Who's there?
Lettuce.
Lettuce who?
Lettuce in, it's cold out here!

What's the difference between a poorly dressed man on a tricycle and a well-dressed man on a bicycle?
Attire.

Knock, knock.
Who's there?
Mustache.
Mustache who?
I mustache you a question, but I'll
shave it for later.

What do you call a lazy kangaroo?
A pouch potato.

I used to be indecisive...
Now I'm not so sure.

Knock, knock.
Who's there?
Donut.
Donut who?
Donut ask, it's a long story.

What's brown and sticky?
A stick.

I told my wife she was drawing her
eyebrows too high.
She looked surprised.

Knock, knock.
Who's there?
Turnip.
Turnip who?
Turnip the heat, it's cold!

Why did the bicycle fall over?
Because it was two-tired.

Knock, knock.
Who's there?
Tennis.
Tennis who?
Tennis the worst knock-knock joke I've
ever heard.

I'm on a whiskey diet.
I've lost three days already.

Knock, knock.
Who's there?
Doris.
Doris who?
Doris locked, that's why I'm knocking!

What do you call an illegally parked
frog?
Toad.

Why do chicken coops only have two doors?
Because if they had four, they'd be a chicken sedan.

Knock, knock.
Who's there?
Bacon.
Bacon who?
Bacon me crazy with all these jokes!

Why don't skeletons fight?
They don't have the guts.

What's the best way to watch a fly fishing tournament?
Live stream.

Knock, knock.
Who's there?
Olive.
Olive who?
Olive you, that's who!

How do you make holy water?
You boil the hell out of it.

I was wondering why the frisbee kept
getting bigger...
Then it hit me.

Knock, knock.
Who's there?
Euripides.
Euripides who?
Euripides pants, you pay for them!

I'm reading a book on anti-gravity.
It's impossible to put down.

Knock, knock.
Who's there?
Boo.
Boo who?
Don't cry, it's just a joke!

I told my wife she should embrace her
mistakes...
So she gave me a hug.

Why do cows wear bells?
Because their horns don't work.

Knock, knock.
Who's there?
Butter.
Butter who?
Butter open the door, I'm freezing!

Did you hear about the circus fire?
It was in tents.

I told my computer I needed a break...
Now it won't stop sending me Kit-Kat
ads.

Knock, knock.
Who's there?
Lettuce.
Lettuce who?
Lettuce in, it's raining out here!

My friend keeps saying "cheer up, man, it could be worse. You could be stuck underground in a hole full of water."
I know he means well.

What do you call a fish wearing a crown?
A kingfish.

Knock, knock.
Who's there?
Lynne.
Lynne who?
Lynne over and I'll tell you!

Why do cows have hooves instead of feet?
Because they lactose.

What did the janitor say when he jumped out of the closet?
Supplies!

Knock, knock.
Who's there?
Yoda-lay-he.
Yoda-lay-he who?
You da-lay-dee who keeps knocking at my door!

What do you get when you cross a snowman with a vampire?
Frostbite.

couldn't figure out why the baseball kept getting bigger...
Then it hit me.

Knock, knock.
Who's there?
Ken.
Ken who?
Ken I come in now?

I once got fired from a canned juice factory.
Apparently, I couldn't concentrate.

I told my wife she was drawing her eyebrows too high.
She looked surprised.

Knock, knock.
Who's there?
Figs.
Figs who?
Figs the doorbell, it's broken!

What's the difference between a hippo and a zippo?
One's heavy, the other's a little lighter.

I would avoid the sushi if I were you...
It's a little fishy.

Knock, knock.
Who's there?
Howard.
Howard who?
Howard you like to hear another joke?

I used to play piano by ear,
But now I use my hands.

What do you call a cow with no legs?
Ground beef.

Knock, knock.
Who's there?
Cow says.
Cow says who?
No, silly, cow says moo!

I gave all my dead batteries away
today...
Free of charge.

What do you call fake spaghetti?
An impasta.

Knock, knock.
Who's there?
Avenue.
Avenue who?
Avenue seen my keys?

I don't play soccer because I enjoy the sport...
I'm just doing it for kicks.

I can't believe I got fired from the calendar factory...
All I did was take a day off.

Knock, knock.
Who's there?
Goat.
Goat who?
Goat to the door and find out!

I used to run a bakery...
But I couldn't make enough dough.

Knock, knock.
Who's there?
Cash.
Cash who?
No thanks, I'll have peanuts.

Why did the chicken join a band?
Because it had the drumsticks.

Knock, knock.
Who's there?
Tank.
Tank who?
You're welcome!

My wife said I should do lunges to stay in shape.
That would be a big step forward.

Knock, knock.
Who's there?
Cash.
Cash who?
No thanks, I'll have peanuts.

Knock, knock.
Who's there?
Broken pencil.
Broken pencil who?
Never mind, it's pointless.

I ordered a chicken and an egg online...
I'll let you know which comes first.

What do you call a bear with no teeth?
A gummy bear.

Knock, knock.
Who's there?
Water.
Water who?
Water you doing knocking on my door?

How do you find Will Smith in the snow?
You look for fresh prints.

Why can't you hear a pterodactyl going to the bathroom?
Because the "P" is silent.

Knock, knock.
Who's there?
Annie.
Annie who?
Annie way you want it, that's the way
you need it!

What's brown and sticky?
A stick.

I got hit in the head with a can of
soda...
Luckily, it was a soft drink.

Knock, knock.
Who's there?
Amos.
Amos who?
A mosquito just bit me!

I used to be a shoe salesman,
But I didn't have enough sole.

Why don't you ever see elephants
hiding in trees?
Because they're so good at it.

Knock, knock.
Who's there?
Scold.
Scold who?
Scold outside, let me in!

I'm terrible at math,
But I can count on my fingers.

Knock, knock.
Who's there?
Noah.
Noah who?
Noah good joke?

Did you hear about the Italian chef
who died?
He pasta way.

What do you call an alligator in a vest?
An investigator.

Knock, knock.
Who's there?
Orange.
Orange who?
Orange you glad I didn't say banana?

I wanted to be a professional skateboarder,
But I couldn't handle the wheels.

Knock, knock.
Who's there?
Justin.
Justin who?
Justin time for more bad jokes!

How do you make a Kleenex dance?
You put a little boogie in it.

I gave my dog a job at the bank...
He's a bark teller.

Knock, knock.
Who's there?
Honeydew.
Honeydew who?
Honeydew you want to hear another joke?

What do you call a bee that can't make up its mind?
A maybe.

Knock, knock.
Who's there?
Juno.
Juno who?
Juno I'm coming over, right?

I was going to make a joke about an elevator...
But it's an uplifting experience.

What did the tomato say to the lettuce
at the race?
Lettuce go!

Knock, knock.
Who's there?
Beets.
Beets who?
Beets me!

What did the sushi say to the bee?
Wasabee!

Why can't bicycles stand up by
themselves?
Because they're two-tired.

Knock, knock.
Who's there?
A little old lady.
A little old lady who?
Wow, I didn't know you could yodel!

I used to be a baker,
But I couldn't make enough dough.

Knock, knock.
Who's there?
Freda.
Freda who?
Freda last joke, you'll laugh for sure!

What did the grape do when it got stepped on?
Nothing, it just let out a little wine.

I used to play piano by ear,
But now I use my hands.

Knock, knock.
Who's there?
Yacht.
Yacht who?
Yacht to know by now!

How do cows stay up to date?
They read the moos-paper.

I can't believe I got fired from the
orange juice factory.
I couldn't concentrate.

Knock, knock.
Who's there?
Dewey.
Dewey who?
Dewey have to keep knocking?

I used to work at a calendar factory,
But I got fired for taking a day off.

Knock, knock.
Who's there?
Luke.
Luke who?
Luke through the peephole and find out!

I told my wife she was drawing her eyebrows too high.
She looked surprised.

Knock, knock.
Who's there?
Justin.
Justin who?
Justin time for more jokes!

I tried to catch some fog earlier.
I mist.

Why did the stadium get hot after the
game?
Because all the fans left.

Knock, knock.
Who's there?
Sven.
Sven who?
Sven you going to laugh at these
jokes?

I only know 25 letters of the alphabet...
I don't know y.

Knock, knock.
Who's there?
Gorilla.
Gorilla who?
Gorilla me a burger, I'm starving!

What did the big flower say to the little flower?
Hey, bud!

I'm on a seafood diet.
I see food and I eat it.

Knock, knock.
Who's there?
Ketchup.
Ketchup who?
Ketchup with me and I'll tell you!

Why did the scarecrow win an
award?
Because he was outstanding in his field

Knock, knock.
Who's there?
Canoe.
Canoe who?
Canoe help me with these jokes?

I used to hate facial hair,
But then it grew on me.

How do you organize a space party?
You planet.

Knock, knock.
Who's there?
Will.
Will who?
Will you ever stop with these jokes?

I told my dog to sit...
But he prefers to lie down.

Knock, knock.
Who's there?
Water.
Water who?
Water you waiting for? Open the door!

What did the blanket say as it fell off the bed?
Oh sheet!

I once ate a watch…
It was time-consuming.

Knock, knock.
Who's there?
Omar.
Omar who?
Omar goodness, these jokes keep coming!

What did the buffalo say to his son when he left for school?
Bison.

Knock, knock.
Who's there?
Iona.
Iona who?
Iona lot of these jokes!

What do you call an elephant that
doesn't matter?
An irrelephant.

Why did the bicycle fall over?
Because it was two-tired.

Knock, knock.
Who's there?
Honeydew.
Honeydew who?
Honeydew you love me?

Why do bees have sticky hair?
Because they use honeycombs.

Knock, knock.
Who's there?
Wanda.
Wanda who?
Wanda hear more jokes?

I just wrote a song about a tortilla...
Actually, it's more of a wrap.

Knock, knock.
Who's there?
Peas.
Peas who?
Peas let me in, I'm cold!

What's green and has wheels?
Grass. I lied about the wheels.

Knock, knock.
Who's there?
Taco.
Taco who?
Taco 'bout bad jokes!

I used to have a job as a waiter,
But it didn't serve me well.

What did one wall say to the other?
I'll meet you at the corner.

Knock, knock.
Who's there?
Adore.
Adore who?
Adore is between us, open up!

Why do cows have hooves instead of feet?
Because they lactose.

Knock, knock.
Who's there?
Dwayne.
Dwayne who?
Dwayne the tub, I'm drowning!

How do you fix a broken pizza?
With tomato paste.

Knock, knock.
Who's there?
Alpaca.
Alpaca who?
Alpaca suitcase, we're going on a trip!

What do you call a snowman with a
six-pack?
An abdominal snowman.

Knock, knock.
Who's there?
Waddle.
Waddle who?
Waddle you know, another joke!

I don't trust stairs...
They're always up to something.

Knock, knock.
Who's there?
Luke.
Luke who?
Luke who's talking now!

What do you call a sad strawberry?
A blueberry.

Why did the golfer bring two pairs of
pants?
In case he got a hole in one.

Knock, knock.
Who's there?
Cereal.
Cereal who?
Cereal-ously, open the door!

I made a belt out of watches once...
It was a waist of time.

Knock, knock.
Who's there?
Hike.
Hike who?
Hike to tell more jokes!

What do you call a lazy kangaroo?
A pouch potato.

Knock, knock.
Who's there?
Kenya.
Kenya who?
Kenya let me in already?

Why did the scarecrow win an award?
Because he was outstanding in his field.

Knock, knock.
Who's there?
Stan.
Stan who?
Stan back, I'm about to tell a joke!

How do you throw a space party?
You planet.

Knock, knock.
Who's there?
Omelette.
Omelette who?
Omelette you in if you stop knocking!

I was going to tell you a joke about an elevator,
But it's an uplifting experience.

Knock, knock.
Who's there?
Sherwood.
Sherwood who?
Sherwood like to tell you a joke!

What's black and white and goes round and round?
A penguin in a revolving door.

Knock, knock.
Who's there?
Earl.
Earl who?
Earl be right back with more jokes!

Knock, knock.
Who's there?
Berry.
Berry who?
Berry nice to meet you!

What kind of shoes do ninjas wear?
Sneakers.

Knock, knock.
Who's there?
Cargo.
Cargo who?
Cargo beep beep!

Why don't skeletons fight each other?
They don't have the guts.

Knock, knock.
Who's there?
Tank.
Tank who?
You're welcome!

What do you call a sleeping bull?
A bulldozer.

Knock, knock.
Who's there?
Police.
Police who?
Police stop telling these jokes!

I used to be afraid of hurdles...
But I got over it.

Knock, knock.
Who's there?
Amish.
Amish who?
Amish you too!

Why don't some couples go to the gym?
Because some relationships don't work out.

Knock, knock.
Who's there?
Doctor.
Doctor who?
Exactly!

Why don't elephants use computers?
Because they're afraid of the mouse.

Knock, knock.
Who's there?
To.
To who?
Actually, it's "to whom."

How does a penguin build its house?
Igloos it together.

Knock, knock.
Who's there?
Hatch.
Hatch who?
Bless you!

What do you call an alligator in a vest?
An investigator.

Knock, knock.
Who's there?
Butter.
Butter who?
Butter let me in, it's cold!

What kind of tree fits in your hand?
A palm tree.

Knock, knock.
Who's there?
Nobel.
Nobel who?
Nobel, that's why I knocked!

What do you call an underwater spy?
James Pond.

Knock, knock.
Who's there?
Tennis.
Tennis who?
Tennis the way I talk!

Why can't your nose be 12 inches long?
Because then it'd be a foot!

Knock, knock.
Who's there?
Olive.
Olive who?
Olive you, that's why I'm here!

Why did the belt get arrested?
It was holding up a pair of pants!

Knock, knock.
Who's there?
A little old lady.
A little old lady who?
Wow, I didn't know you could yodel!

Why don't vampires go to barbecues?
They don't like steak.

Knock, knock.
Who's there?
Harry.
Harry who?
Harry up, I have more jokes!

What do you call a magic dog?
A labracadabrador.

Knock, knock.
Who's there?
Snow.
Snow who?
Snow body knows the answer!

What do you call a fish with no eyes?
Fsh.

Knock, knock.
Who's there?
Boo.
Boo who?
Don't cry, it's just a joke!

Why did the math book look sad?
Because it had too many problems.

Knock, knock.
Who's there?
Doughnut.
Doughnut who?
Doughnut you want to hear more
jokes?

What do you call a man with no nose
and no body?
Nobody knows.

Why couldn't the bicycle stand up by
itself?
It was two-tired.

Knock, knock.
Who's there?
Leaf.
Leaf who?
Leaf me alone, I'm tired!

How do you catch a squirrel?
Climb a tree and act like a nut.

Knock, knock.
Who's there?
Harry.
Harry who?
Harry up and answer!

What do you call a fish that wears a crown?
A kingfish.

Knock, knock.
Who's there?
Brittany.
Brittany who?
Brittany me one more joke and I'll laugh!

What do you get when you cross a
vampire and a snowman?
Frostbite.

Knock, knock.
Who's there?
Dozen.
Dozen who?
Dozen anybody want to hear my
jokes?

Why was the broom late to the
meeting?
It swept in.

Knock, knock.
Who's there?
Eddie.
Eddie who?
Eddie body want to hear another
joke?

What's brown and sounds like a bell?
Dung!

Knock, knock.
Who's there?
Cow says.
Cow says who?
No, silly, cow says moo!

Why don't you ever see elephants
hiding in trees?
Because they're so good at it.

Knock, knock.
Who's there?
Hawaii.
Hawaii who?
Hawaii you doing today?

What's the difference between a poorly dressed man on a unicycle and a well-dressed man on a bicycle?
Attire.

Knock, knock.
Who's there?
Cargo.
Cargo who?
Cargo beep beep!

How do you fix a broken tomato?
With tomato paste.

Knock, knock.
Who's there?
Howard.
Howard who?
Howard you like another joke?

Why did the cookie go to the doctor?
Because it felt crummy.

Knock, knock.
Who's there?
Luke.
Luke who?
Luke who's telling more jokes!

Why don't some couples go to the gym?
Because some relationships don't work out.

Knock, knock.
Who's there?
Wendy.
Wendy who?
Wendy you ever stop telling jokes?

I got hit in the head with a can of soda...
Luckily it was a soft drink.

Knock, knock.
Who's there?
Tank.
Tank who?
Tank you for laughing!

What's orange and sounds like a parrot?
A carrot.

Knock, knock.
Who's there?
Sven.
Sven who?
Sven are you going to start laughing?

Why can't you hear a pterodactyl
going to the bathroom?
Because the "P" is silent.

Knock, knock.
Who's there?
Anita.
Anita who?
Anita break from these jokes!

What do you get when you cross a
snowman with a vampire?
Frostbite.

Knock, knock.
Who's there?
Voodoo.
Voodoo who?
Voodoo you think you are, telling all
these jokes?

What did the fisherman say to the
magician?
Pick a cod, any cod.

Knock, knock.
Who's there?
Toby.
Toby who?
Toby or not Toby, that is the question.

How do you organize a space party?
You planet.

Knock, knock.
Who's there?
Goliath.
Goliath who?
Goliath down, you look tired!

What do you call a group of musical whales?
An orca-stra.

Knock, knock.
Who's there?
Icy.
Icy who?
Icy you're still telling jokes!

Knock, knock.
Who's there?
Rufus.
Rufus who?
Rufus leaking, better fix it!

Why did the scarecrow win an award?
Because he was outstanding in his field.

What did one snowman say to the other?
Do you smell carrots?

Knock, knock.
Who's there?
Donut.
Donut who?
Donut ask me, I'm just telling jokes!

Why don't fish play basketball?
Because they're afraid of the net.

Knock, knock.
Who's there?
Dishes.
Dishes who?
Dishes a bad joke!

Why did the chicken join a band?
Because it had the drumsticks.

Knock, knock.
Who's there?
Harry.
Harry who?
Harry up, we're almost done!

Why don't skeletons fight each other?
They don't have the guts.

Knock, knock.
Who's there?
Omelette.
Omelette who?
Omelette smarter than you think!

Why did the golfer bring two pairs of pants?
In case he got a hole in one.

Knock, knock.
Who's there?
Earl.
Earl who?
Earl be seeing you soon with more jokes!

Why did the tomato turn red?
Because it saw the salad dressing!

Knock, knock.
Who's there?
Cash.
Cash who?
No thanks, I prefer peanuts!

What do you call a factory that makes good products?
A satisfactory.

Knock, knock.
Who's there?
Figs.
Figs who?
Figs the doorbell, it's broken!

How do you make holy water?
You boil the hell out of it.

Knock, knock.
Who's there?
Hatch.
Hatch who?
Bless you!

Why did the coffee file a police report?
It got mugged.

Knock, knock.
Who's there?
Alpaca.
Alpaca who?
Alpaca the suitcase, we're going on vacation!

What do you call an alligator in a vest?
An investigator.

Knock, knock.
Who's there?
Control freak.
Control freak who?
Okay, now you say "Control freak who?"

Made in the USA
Las Vegas, NV
08 December 2024

13243660R00059